Acknowledgments

For permission to use copyright material acknowledgment is made to
the following:
For the extracts from the diary of Francis Kilvert to Jonathan Cape Ltd;
for 'Condormouse' from *Who's Zoo* by Conrad Aiken to the author and
Jonathan Cape Ltd; for 'Small Singing' from *The Book of Small* by Emily
Carr to the author and Clarke Irwin and Co Ltd; for 'My Brother Gets
Letters' from *Wouldn't You Like to Know* by Michael Rosen and 'In the
Daytime' from *Mind Your Own Business* by Michael Rosen to the author
and Andre Deutsch Ltd; for 'Blondin's Rainbow' from *Winter's Tales*
to the author, Judith Vidal Hall; for 'Iron Hawk tells of General Custer's
Last Stand' from *Black Elk Speaks* by John G. Neihardt and the John G.
Neihardt Trust; for 'The Gay Goshawk' from *Thou Shalt Not Suffer
Witches* by Dorothy K. Haynes to the author and Methuen and Co Ltd;
for 'Assignment with an Octopus' from *A Pattern of Islands* by Arthur
Grimble to the author and John Murray (Publishers) Ltd; for 'A Perfect
Liar' from *Armenian Folk Tales and Fables* translated by Charles Downing
to the translator and reprinted by permission of Oxford University
Press; for 'The Golden Kite, the Silver Wind' from *The Flying Machine*
by Ray Bradbury to the author and A. D. Peters and Co Ltd; for
'January, February, March' and 'October, November, December' to
Geoffrey Summerfield; for 'Do Not Be Afraid' from *The Way to Rainy
Mountain* by N. Scott Momaday to the author and The University of
New Mexico Press, Albuquerque.

Every effort has been made to trace owners of copyright material, but in
some cases this has not proved possible. The publishers would be glad to
hear from any further copyright owners of material reproduced in
Tales 5.

Contents

TALES
FIVE

a collection of stories
chosen by

GEOFFREY
SUMMERFIELD

WLE Ward Lock Educational

ISBN 0 7062 3722 6 paperback
ISBN 0 7062 3782 X hardback

First published 1978
Reprinted 1980

Cover by Ruth Orbach

Filmset in 'Monophoto' Bembo
by Servis Filmsetting Ltd, Manchester
and printed by Robert MacLehose and Company Limited, Glasgow
for Ward Lock Educational
116 Baker Street, London WIM 2BB
A member of the Pentos Group

Made in Great Britain

January, February, March,
Freeze, stiff as starch,
Flakes blow, cheeks glow,
Feet trudge slow, through the snow.

Blondin's Rainbow

There was once a man called Blondin. He could walk higher and finer than any man in the world. So high and fine was his walking that he thought he would try the most difficult walk ever made, the highest and finest of any man. A wire was stretched tight and high, and a thousand feet long, above the waters of Niagara in the U.S.A., the highest, deepest waterfall in the world. Blondin walks again!

For it was not the first time that Blondin had come to Niagara. He had been here before. He had done all that it was possible to do. He had wheeled wheelbarrows on his wire across the Falls; carried men on his back – men who trusted him; blindfolded without his eyes; on stilts that rocked as he walked. And finally, his most spectacular achievement of all, he had made and eaten an omelette there in the middle of his wire. He had carried his eggs and eaten them all. The crowds had gone wild with the joy and suspense.

And now here he was again. The hopes of the crowd were high, though their imagination failed. 'What would it be this time?' they asked themselves. 'What could he do that he had not already done?' Standing excitedly in the thin drizzle which had begun to fall they watched the arrival of the great man. 'A little older,' they said. 'A bit too old, perhaps, for this sort of thing. You have to know when to stop: quit whilst there's still time.' They

shook their heads quietly, and raised quizzical
eyebrows. Many of them were privately certain that
he would not make it this time. He was fatter, more
bulging in the calf, and his famous twirled
moustache looked a little sad. But maybe he had
learned a new trick or two, and they looked forward
to some new and dazzling feat about to be performed above their heads, never believing for one
minute that the wire alone could be enough, be it as
high as never was. That, they thought, would be a
cheat and disappointment. They hadn't travelled all
those miles in the rain and early morning just for
that. But they needn't worry, they decided. This was
Blondin. And they cheered him as he stepped
amongst them.

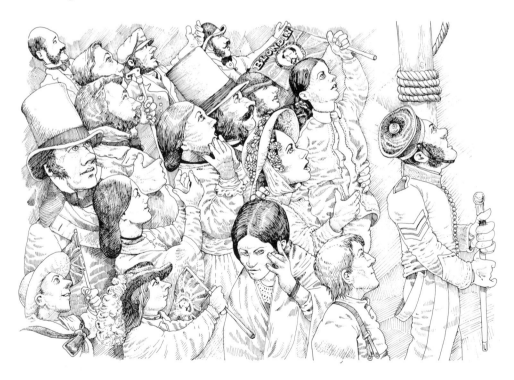

Indeed, all over Europe they had not ceased to cheer him. In circus rings, as high over the sawdust as it was possible to be, the lights above dazzling the eyes of those below, they had lifted up their faces to watch him, silent and intent. No one breathed. The children, or some of them, shut their eyes as he started out. Some stuffed their fists, tightly clenched, into their mouths to hold down a scream that might leak out. Others pushed their longest finger into each ear to keep out the crash. But there was never a crash. Every time the breathing which had stopped started again in a great sigh which rippled round the ring. The eyes opened, the fists and fingers came out to clap, and the new found voices cheered for all they were worth. 'Blondin! Blondin!'

They came from miles to see him in fairgrounds, circuses, music-halls. His name was in the brightest lights: he headed every bill. But still, it seemed, for him it was not enough. 'I must get higher; stretch the wire finer.' He was never satisfied. He out-topped the biggest Big Top, and walked on his wire in the highest buildings men could offer. He even performed in magical palaces of glass over the heads of royalty, turned somersaults over them in air in the soaring glass cage. Steadily and elegantly he walked and performed. His precarious balance looked like security to those who watched from below. They marvelled, and praised him all over the world. His life history appeared in the newspapers. They made up songs about him and sold them on the streets. And so he had finally come to Niagara to dance for them on his wire; to amaze and startle them with his tricks.

Now here he was again – Niagara. He had crossed the Ocean to walk once more. He had to do it though he didn't exactly know why. It wasn't that he particularly wanted to any more, because it was true that he was old and tired now – perhaps was losing his skill. But it was there, and would remain there as long as he could put one foot forward onto a tight-rope. And this one time now, with the wire at its new and impossibly dizzy height, was the most important moment in his life. This time was different from all the occasions in the past. Only Blondin knew. There would be no tricks this time. He was done with crowds. The cheers no longer mattered. He'd had those all his life as long as he could remember. This time there was just Blondin and his wire, higher than ever before, higher than even he had imagined. The waters seemed further and deeper than he had ever known, yet so near, and for almost the first time in his life, so easy to fall into. He looked at the wire and was afraid. The terrible drop between the wire and the deeps below was a gap he could feel. Never had he thought to know this within himself. Others had spoken of it before climbing to their wires and trapezes, but not Blondin.

As he looked, his past triumphs seemed to melt away. Nothing he'd done before mattered any longer, and to make things worse, he no longer knew if he could make it across his wire this time. He thought about the things he might do instead. Change his act altogether, perhaps, or just stop, give up, retire, unsurpassed in the eyes of the world. He'd earned a rest, and he'd made enough money in his performing life to live comfortably for the rest of it. But somehow he couldn't do that yet. This was the only real thing left to him, and he just had to get across for the last time. It wasn't simply that the wire was higher than ever before, nor that the Falls seemed so impossibly long down. He had to conquer the gap that filled his mind and made him tremble, so that his knees wouldn't stop jumping of their own accord, and his toes twitched on the red carpet with which they had paved his way to the wire.

The crowd had grown bigger than ever. Someone had spread the story that this was to be the last time: Blondin's swan-song. He'd never perform again, whether he crossed the wire or not. They whispered that it was all or nothing with him, and waited impatiently for something to happen. They had come from all over the countryside, people who had heard of this man, had not believed, had laughed incredulously, and now had come to see for themselves. Most of them had never set foot on a wire, had never climbed higher than the fencing which surrounded their chicken-runs at home. But there were, too, those who had dreamed of the high-wire in moments of time, and who regretted never having tested its strength with their own. They had come to see and experience at secondhand the thrills they had missed. There were the sceptics who had come to see him fall; the simple who came to be entertained. Finally there were the old 'Pros', his brothers in the art, who had walked the tight-rope themselves, and now had come to watch with wise eyes the performance of their acknowledged master. These were the ones who walked the wire with him, who knew the taste in his mouth and the tightness of his throat. They would have held his hands and helped him over if they could, but they knew the aloneness, that it could be no other than it was. Besides, this was higher than any of them had ever reached; they had retired before Niagara.

Blondin walked up to where the thin silver wire stretched away from him over the emptiness beneath and the deeps below. Then he walked on further along the cliff top to look over into this great abyss. He saw the boiling crashing waters far, far below him. They thrashed and beat on the tumbled rocks at the bottom, and broke into white

13

foaming fragments. Everything was confused and half-hidden by the glittering spray which shot back up from the shattering.

The crowd gasped. How could he bear to look? Everybody knew that heights were all right as long as you never looked down. It wasn't good to know how steep the drop, how terrible the fall, the crash at the bottom. It was better to keep your eyes fixed ahead, to look up even. Only then could you keep your mind empty of the drop. Not to know what lay beneath was the only possible way to succeed.

But Blondin knew what waited for him down there. He had seen it before, though never so clearly as now and it had filled his mind for years. Now he leaned far out over the edge to stare, only confirming what he had always known. The broken rocks and crashing water, the steep drop through emptiness, the gap between here and there, were more real in his mind than in his eyes as he looked.

He got up from where he had been hanging over the edge. Better get on with it. He felt a little stiff from the wetness of the air around him, and his knees cracked from the cold damp of the earth. It wasn't a good day. Indeed his manager, on arriving at the site, had strongly urged him not to attempt the crossing that day; to come back tomorrow, the next day, any day – so long as it was calm and still. But for Blondin it was the only day. As he waited he knew that the time had come. This was the right day for him, and he couldn't wait any longer.

He was not unduly troubled by the clouds that hung low and grey in the sky, nor by the coldness in his joints. A thin mist had gathered above the Falls, and in the middle swallowed up the wire so that it seemed not to be there. The thin wire stretched so tight and high reached out into nothingness: stopped in mid-air. He could see no end, and it seemed too, that to walk into invisibility might result in his stepping into the gap. 'Don't go. Don't go,' his manager urged. 'Of course, it's a pity to disappoint the crowd, but they'll come back. They always do. Anything for a thrill.' Privately, the crowd was thinking not of the walk, but of a fall. They felt a strange tension as the thought of tragedy touched them. They became restless with suppressed excitement and anticipation. Now they were urging a decision one way or the other. Some, like the manager, urged prudence, another day. Others, unwilling to be cheated of the spectacle, shouted at Blondin to 'Get on with it!'

The manager, wrapped up fatly in his great coat with the tight belt and fur collar, so enveloped he could scarcely move his arms, felt strongly about risking his prize exhibit. This was his livelihood after all, and had he not the right to grow fatter yet on Blondin's back? Yet still Blondin knew. Here was now, and he must go over or never. It worried him a little that the wire disappeared, that the opposite cliff was invisible. Worse still was the wind. It wasn't felt all the time, but blew spasmodically in sharp gusts which opened coats and snatched hats. It could be nasty, he thought, to meet that halfway across. It could upset the poise, whip up the ends of his pole on which he relied so strongly to retain his

balance. The pole itself could become a danger.
Still, he knew the wire was there, had seen it glint-
ing in the sun the day before, thin and fine, but
securely fixed and there all the way over. Now it
hummed slightly, and sang into the wind. He felt a
deep fondness for his wire warming him. He longed
to be nothing else than he was. He would go.
Nobody should stop him. The crowd was unim-
portant. He was alone. Blondin and his wire. The
chaotic waters beneath, most of all that long gap,
were his. Not even the thought of his manager,
anxiously puffing out clouds of steam and stamping
his feet, could make any difference. He liked him
well enough. Jolly fellow, and a great help on the
business side, the organisation, the money. He'd set
the whole thing up out there. But well – he wasn't
walking. It wasn't his wire.

Blondin stretched out his hand for the pole that
would help him in his walk. It was thin and long
and undulating as he grasped it firmly in both hands
stretched out before him. He was ready to walk. He
set his foot on the wire, bouncing it up and down to
get the mood of it, to accustom his feet to its
familiar feel. It was all right: firm, tense, and there
all the way. The crowd was disappointed he didn't
turn and wave. They would have liked to cheer.
Poor showmanship. Things like that looked bad in a
public performer. They did not know, how could
they, that for Blondin they simply were not there.
He had begun what he came for. Now there was
only the wire, the broken deep below, the space
between – together with the cold wind inside. He

16

must reach the other side, and he would.

He took his first step forward. The wire began to move and sway beneath him as it always did. He was used to that. He bobbed and balanced as he stood there. The wind still troubled him. A cold eddy took the ends of the pole and whipped them up and down in its breath. Dangerous. Better to be rid of it now than be clinging on at the wrong moment. The pole fell silently, slowly, swiftly down. There was an exclamation from the crowd. The fat manager let out a strangled scream which was lost in the thunder of the waters. Blondin didn't hear. He felt better without the pole. Now it was really just him. He would do better than he thought: be more alone than he had imagined. He stretched out his arms rigidly on each side, looked straight and firm across to the invisible other side, and slowly at first, then almost trippingly, set out.

His feet slid their way along the wire, smoothly feeling out their path. He was light and could have danced. It didn't matter, he told himself, that he couldn't see the wire further on. His feet could feel it and that was all that mattered. In any case, maybe the mist would clear before he got there. It might not even cover much of the wire, and he would soon be through. He went on forward.

Now he was approaching the mist. His feet continued, but the grey folds were cold and wet. It was a sheet thrown over his head to confuse and hamper his movements. Yet still he was all right. He knew his wire and trusted his feet. His arms swayed each side of him like twin vanes. But now the wire began to twitch and sway treacherously. A wind inside the fog swirled it around him, hanging damp obscure folds over him, baffling his senses as it closed tighter on him. He couldn't go on. The wind and fog were too strong against him. Into his mind came the thought of turning back whilst he still could. Perhaps it would be wiser after all. No one would blame him under conditions like these. They'd even cheer, probably. 'Never mind, Blondin, you'll do it yet.' He saw the droop of his moustache as he stepped on to firm land, felt the shame in his eyes. The crowd parted to let him through, comforting him as he passed. Their respect for his earlier triumphs would be unimpaired. For Blondin it was the feeling of defeat. It was there, then gone. Blondin felt no more. He knew there was no going back. To turn in the fog and wind was impossible.

His mind was a stone. His feet were numb and unfeeling on the wire. It was dark, and he couldn't go forward. He twitched and swayed with the wire in the effort to retain his precarious balance. Only that unfelt determination kept him upright. Not even the long gap was in his mind, though somewhere deep was the knowledge that if he had to fall he would. Better that than go back. Blondin stood and waited. He was high over nothing, hidden by fog in the middle of his wire. In his mind he was in the water below, broken on the rocks. He had fallen through the gap.

On the side from which he had started the crowd had watched him disappear. A few drifted away, knowing they would not see him arrive at the other

side. They were cold for their homes and firesides.
The rest remained, waiting around for something
they didn't know what. Though the far cliff was
invisible, someone, they were sure, would send
word what had happened. Maybe the cheers would
echo back from the other side. In any case, you
couldn't just leave someone out on a limb like that.
No, better stay and see.

On the far side the expectant unknowing crowd
stared hard with reddening eyes and cold hands.
They tried to peer into the heart of the fog, hoping
to see a small wraith emerging towards them. They

strained to see, and it seemed a long time. There was nothing there yet. They looked at watches and knew that it was taking too long. It was getting late. Either he hadn't started (and you couldn't blame him really; it was a foul day), or . . . Just then the message filtered through that Blondin was on his way. They stretched their eyes further into the swirling fog which seemed at moments to part, only to come together again more impenetrably than before. There was nothing there. The wind was trying to blow away the clouds, but it would certainly blow away Blondin too, if it hadn't already.

The long silent minutes ticked by. They began to be afraid: to fear for Blondin, that something had happened to him. He couldn't come now. No one, not even the Maestro, could hang that long in air. It was all over. Yet they hadn't heard a cry. Maybe the wind had blown it back to the other side, or the noise of the waters drowned it. The fear that the worst had happened grew. No eyes met, though they no longer looked out from their end of the wire. The crowd was restless. They didn't know what to do. No one spoke, except the children who still expected the great man to appear at any moment and couldn't understand why there were tears in the grown-up eyes. 'When's he coming, Papa?' 'Mama, where is he?' 'Come on Blondin!' 'We want Blondin!' Their parents hushed them from above. It was all a bit puzzling. Perhaps he wasn't coming today after all. Perhaps he'd turned back. They hoped not, because they loved Blondin, the pictures and photographs they had seen of the funny little man. Well, it was hard luck, but he'd come some day they believed. Even if it could not be Blondin there were other men with wires and poles. They, better than the grown-ups, knew the problems. For hadn't they, many of them, practised on the wire fences around the place? They'd had some bangs and bruises, even broken arms and legs, at which their parents had drawn the line and forbidden such dangerous games. Still there were a few who secretly went on practising, and could not give up until the day when they too would be walking over Niagara. But the parents knew that Blondin had fallen, had failed, was by now dead. And they could not bring themselves to tell their children.

Blondin on the wire stood. And he stood, and he stood. And the cold stone in his mind sank as the wind parted the fog and whipped up the cold folds from his shoulders. A thin silver thread stretched once more in front of him. His feet began to move forward of their own accord, lightly and calmly. Blondin, arms straight out, head high, walked forward again, unseeing to the other side.

The crowd who had stopped looking, who despaired, saw a grey shadow. It couldn't be! It was! No! It wasn't possible! He must have gone down by this time! – But yes! It was, it really was! He was coming! He was through! A great cheer began, but was broken before it hit the air. He hadn't actually arrived yet, had he? Plenty could happen between here and there. Many a slip and all. The slightest mistake at any moment on the wire slippery with wetness, and the wind even stronger now, could cause disaster. But he was coming – and fast too. Heavens, the man was mad! He was actually running! He wasn't down. Here he came. There was a gasp of horror as his arms swirled wildly. He was nearly with them now. He was going to do it. They couldn't believe it, but were immeasurably glad. Hands reached out ready to grasp him. He'd made it. He'd arrived. He was here.

A great cheer, unchecked this time, welcomed him. 'Blondin! Blondin! Hurrah! Hurrah!' And Blondin, cold and wet from the water which had splashed him, and the dampness which had soaked beneath his skin, stood weary and exhausted on land again. Firm wet brown and green land stretched either side of the second red carpet. He'd done it. He looked back. The mist had lifted, blown up on the wind. The thin silver line stretched all the way back to the other side. He could see the crowd there leaping and waving – cheering too, no doubt. Blondin smiled. He smiled a smile that was weary, but happy and wise too, because he'd crossed the tight-rope, and knew that never again would he have to fall into the abyss, the waters.

As he looked he saw what he had never seen before, the bridge that spanned the waterfall. It shone and glowed in all its colours. The spray glittered and was transformed in the light. It arced over the churning below, complete from side to side. Curious. It was always there. He'd just never noticed it before.

Judith Vidal

Extracts from Kilvert's Diary

Saturday, Christmas Eve

An intense frost in the night. Lowest point 14
degrees, F. When I went in to my bath I sat down
amongst a shoal of fragments of broken floating ice
as sharp as glass. Everything was frozen stiff and
stark, sponge, brushes and all. After I had used the
sponge and put it into the basin it was frozen to the
basin again in less than 5 minutes.

Sunday, Christmas Day

As I lay awake praying in the early morning I thought I heard a sound of distant bells. It was an intense frost. I sat down in my bath upon a sheet of thick ice which broke in the middle into large pieces whilst sharp points and jagged edges stuck all round the sides of the tub like *chevaux de frise*, not particularly comforting to the naked thighs and loins, for the keen ice cut like broken glass. The ice water stung and scorched like fire. I had to collect the floating pieces of ice and pile them on a chair before I could use the sponge and then I had to thaw the sponge in my hands for it was a mass of ice.

Monday, 28 November

Old James Jones told me how he was once travelling
from Hereford to Hay by coach when the coach
was wrecked in a flood by Bredwardine Bridge
because the coachman would not take the bearing
reins of the horses off. The bearing reins kept the
horses' noses down under water, they plunged and
reared and got the coach off the road and swimming
like a boat, and an old lady inside screaming
horribly, 'Don't keep such a noise, Ma'am,' said old
Jones, throwing himself off the roof into a hedge-
row against which the coach was swept by the fierce
current. 'We won't leave you before we get you out
somehow.' He was followed by most of the
passengers on the roof, though one very tall man
fell into the water on his face all along like a log,
and waded through the flood out onto the Bredwardine side. One outside passenger was a miller of
the neighbourhood who had a boat on the river.
This was sent for and the old lady pacified and
pulled into it through the coach window. The
coachman was prayed and entreated to loose the
bearing reins, but refused to do it. Two horses were
drowned, one wheeler went down under the pole.
The other, a leader, broke loose and plunged and
pawed and reared at the bridge out of the flood till
he was exhausted, and then fell over backwards into
the stream and was rolled away by the current.

Francis Kilvert

Iron Hawk tells of General Custer's Last Stand

I am a Hunkpapa, and, as I told you before, I was fourteen years old. The sun was overhead and more, but I was eating my first meal that day, because I had been sleeping. While I was eating I heard the crier saying: 'The chargers are coming.' I jumped up and rushed out to our horses. They were grazing close to camp. I roped one, and the others stampeded, but my older brother had caught his horse already and headed the others off. When I got on my horse with the rope hitched around his nose, the soldiers were shooting up there and people were running and men and boys were catching their horses that were scared because of the shooting and yelling. I saw little children running up from the river where they had been swimming; and all the women and children were running down the valley.

Our horses stampeded down toward the Minneconjous, but we rounded them up again and brought them back. By now warriors were running toward the soldiers, and getting on the ponies, and many of the Hunkpapas were gathering in the brush and timber near the place where the soldiers had stopped and got off their horses. I rode past a very old man who was shouting: 'Boys, take courage! Would you see these little children taken away from me like dogs?'

I went into our tepee and got dressed for war as fast as I could; but I could hear bullets whizzing outside, and I was so shaky that it took me a long time to braid an eagle feather into my hair. Also, I had to hold my pony's rope all the time, and he kept jerking me and trying to get away. While I was doing this, crowds of warriors on horses were roaring by up stream, yelling: 'Hoka hey!' Then I rubbed red paint all over my face and took my bow and arrows and got on my horse. I did not have a gun, only a bow and arrows.

When I was on my horse, the fight up stream seemed to be over, because everybody was starting back downstream and yelling: 'It's a good day to die!' Soldiers were coming at the other end of the village, and nobody knew how many there were down there.

A man by the name of Little Bear rode up to me on a pinto horse, and he had a very pretty saddle blanket. He said: 'Take courage, boy! The earth is all that lasts!' So I rode fast with him and the others downstream, and many of us Hunkpapas gathered on the east side of the river at the foot of a gulch that led back up the hill where the second soldier band (Custer's) was. There was a very brave Shyela with us, and I heard someone say: 'He is going!' I looked, and it was this Shyela. He had on a spotted war bonnet and a spotted robe made of some animal's skin and this was fastened with a spotted belt. He was going up the hill alone and we all followed part way. There were soldiers along the ridge up there and they were on foot holding their horses. The Shyela rode right close to them in a circle several times and all the soldiers shot at him.

Then he rode back to where we had stopped at the head of the gulch. He was saying: 'Ah, ah!' Someone said: 'Shyela friend, what is the matter?' He began undoing his spotted belt, and when he shook it, bullets dropped out. He was very sacred and the soldiers could not hurt him. He was a fine looking man.

We stayed there awhile waiting for something and there was shooting everywhere. Then I heard a voice crying: 'Now they are going, they are going!' We looked up and saw the cavalry horses stampeding. These were all grey horses.

I saw Little Bear's horse rear and race up hill toward the soldiers. When he got close, his horse was shot out from under him, and he got up limping because the bullet went through his leg; and he started hobbling back to us with the soldiers shooting at him. His brother-friend, Elk Nation, went up there on his horse and took Little Bear behind him and rode back safe with bullets striking all around him. It was his duty to go to his brother-friend even if he knew he would be killed.

By now a big cry was going up all around the soldiers up there and the warriors were coming from everywhere and it was getting dark with dust and smoke.

We saw soldiers start running down hill right towards us. Nearly all of them were afoot, and I think they were so scared that they didn't know what they were doing. They were making their arms go as though they were running very fast, but they were only walking. Some of them shot their

guns in the air. We all yelled 'Hoka hey!' and
charged toward them, riding all around them in the
twilight that had fallen on us.

I met a soldier on horseback, and I let him have
it. The arrow went through from side to side under
his ribs and it stuck out on both sides. He screamed
and took hold of his saddle horn and hung on,
wobbling, with his head hanging down. I kept
along beside him, and I took my heavy bow and
struck him across the back of the neck. He fell from
his saddle, and I got off and beat him to death with
my bow. I kept on beating him awhile after he was
dead, and every time I hit him I said 'Hownh!' I
was mad, because I was thinking of the women and
little children running down there, all scared and out
of breath. These Wasichus wanted it, and they came
to get it, and we gave it to them. I did not see much
more. I saw Brings Plenty kill a soldier with a war
club. I saw Red Horn Buffalo fall. There was a
Lakota riding along the edge of the gulch, and he
was yelling to look out, that there was a soldier
hiding in there. I saw him charge in and kill the
soldier and begin slashing him with a knife.

Then we began to go towards the river, and the
dust was lifting so that we could see the women and
children coming over to us from across the river.
The soldiers were all rubbed out there and scattered
around.

The women swarmed up the hill and began stripping the soldiers. They were yelling and laughing
and singing now. I saw something funny. Two fat
old women were stripping a soldier, who was

wounded and playing dead. When they had him naked, he jumped up and began fighting with the two fat women. He was swinging one of them around, while the other was trying to stab him with her knife. After a while, another woman rushed up and shoved her knife into him and he died really dead. It was funny to see the naked Wasichu fighting with the fat women.

By now we saw that our warriors were all charging on some soldiers that had come from the hill up river to help the second band that we had rubbed out. They ran back and we followed, chasing them up on their hill again where they had their pack mules. We could not hurt them much there, because they had been digging to hide themselves and they were lying behind saddles and other things. I was down by the river and I saw some soldiers come down there with buckets. They had no guns, just buckets. Some boys were down there, and they came out of the brush and threw mud and rocks in the soldiers' faces and chased them into the river. I guess they got enough to drink, for they are drinking yet. We killed them in the water.

Afterwhile it was nearly sundown, and I went home with many others to eat, while some others stayed to watch the soldiers on the hill. I hadn't eaten all day, because the trouble started just when I was beginning to eat my first meal.

John Neihardt

A Witty Answer

A certain king was angry with one of his lords and put him in prison; wishing to keep him there, he said he would only set him free if he could bring to the court a horse which was neither grey nor black, brown nor bay, white nor roan, dun, chestnut, nor piebald – and, in short, the king enumerated every possible colour that a horse could be. The imprisoned lord promised to get such a horse if the king would set him free at once. As soon as he was at liberty the lord asked the king to send a groom for the horse, but begged that the groom might come neither on Monday nor Tuesday, Wednesday nor Thursday, Friday, Saturday, nor Sunday, but on any other day of the week that suited His Majesty.

Georgian folk tale

The Loaded Dog

Dave Regan, Jim Bently, and Andy Page were sinking a shaft at Stony Creek in search of a rich gold quartz reef which was supposed to exist in the vicinity. There is always a rich reef supposed to exist in the vicinity; the only questions are whether it is ten feet or hundreds beneath the surface, and in which direction. They had struck some pretty solid rock, also water which kept them baling. They used the old-fashioned blasting-powder and time-fuse. They'd make a sausage or cartridge of blasting-powder in a skin of strong calico or canvas, get the drill-hole as dry as possible, drop in the cartridge with some dry dust, and wad and ram with stiff clay and broken brick. Then they'd light the fuse and get out of the hole and wait. The result was usually an ugly pot-hole in the bottom of the shaft and half a barrow-load of broken rock.

There was plenty of fish in the creek, fresh-water bream, cod, cat-fish, and tailers. The party were fond of fish, and Andy and Dave of fishing. Andy would fish for three hours at a stretch if encouraged by a 'nibble' or a 'bite' now and then – say once in twenty minutes. The butcher was always willing to give meat in exchange for fish when they caught more than they could eat; but now it was winter, and these fish wouldn't bite. However, the creek was low, just a chain of muddy waterholes, from the hole with a few bucketfuls in it to the sizable pool with an average depth of six or seven feet, and they could get fish by bailing out the smaller holes or muddying up the water in the larger ones till the fish rose to the surface. There was the cat-fish, with spikes growing out of the sides of its head, and if you got pricked you'd know it, as Dave said. Andy took off his boots, tucked up his trousers, and went into a hole one day to stir up the mud with his feet, and he knew it. Dave scooped one out with his hand and got pricked, and he knew it too; his arm swelled, and the pain throbbed up into his shoulder, and down into his stomach too, he said, like a toothache he had once, and kept him awake for two nights – only the toothache pain had a 'burred edge', Dave said.

Dave got an idea.

'Why not blow the fish up in the big waterhole with a cartridge?' he said. 'I'll try it.'

He thought the thing out and Andy Page worked it out. Andy usually put Dave's theories into practice if they were practicable, or bore the blame for the failure and the chaffing of his mates if they weren't.

He made a cartridge about three times the size of those they used in the rock. Jim Bently said it was big enough to blow the bottom out of the river. The idea was to sink the cartridge in the water with the open end of the fuse attached to a float on the surface, ready for lighting. Andy dipped the cartridge in melted bees-wax to make it watertight. 'We'll have to leave it some time before we light it,' said Dave, 'to give the fish time to get over their

34

scare when we put it in, and come nosing round
again; so we'll want it well watertight.'

Round the cartridge Andy, at Dave's suggestion,
bound a strip of sail canvas. Dave's schemes were
elaborate, and he often worked his inventions out to
nothing. The cartridge was rigid and solid enough
now, but Andy and Dave wanted to be sure. Andy
sewed on another layer of canvas, and stood it
carefully against a tent-peg, where he'd know where
to find it, and wound the fuse loosely round it. Then
he went to the camp-fire to try some potatoes which
were boiling in their jackets in a billy, and to see
about frying some chops for dinner. Dave and Jim
were at work in the claim that morning.

They had a big black young retriever dog – or rather an overgrown pup, a big, foolish, four-footed mate, who was always slobbering round them and lashing their legs with his heavy tail that swung round like a stock-whip. Most of his head was usually a red, idiotic slobbering grin of appreciation of his own silliness. He seemed to take life, the world, his two-legged mates, and his own instinct as a huge joke. He'd retrieve anything; he carted back most of the camp rubbish that Andy threw away. They had a cat that died in hot weather, and Andy threw it a good distance away in the scrub; and early one morning the dog found the cat, after it had been dead a week or so, and carried it back to camp, and laid it just inside the tent-flaps, where it could best make its presence known when the mates should rise and begin to sniff suspiciously in the sickly smothering atmosphere of the summer sun-rise. He used to retrieve them when they went in swimming; he'd jump in after them, and take their hands in his mouth, and try to swim out with them, and scratch their naked bodies with his paws. They loved him for his good-heartedness and his foolish-ness, but when they wished to enjoy a swim they had to tie him up in camp.

He watched Andy with great interest all the morning making the cartridge, and hindered him considerably, trying to help; but about noon he went off to the claim to see how Dave and Jim were getting on, and to come home to dinner with them. Andy saw them coming, and put a panful of mutton-chops on the fire. Andy was cook to-day;

Dave and Jim stood with their backs to the fire, as bushmen do in all weathers, waiting till dinner should be ready. The retriever went nosing round after something he seemed to have missed.

Andy's brain still worked on the cartridge; his eye was caught by the glare of an empty kerosene-tin lying in the bushes, and it struck him that it wouldn't be a bad idea to sink the cartridge packed with clay, sand, or stones in the tin, to increase the force of the explosion. He may have been all out, from a scientific point of view, but the notion looked all right to him. Jim Bently, by the way, wasn't interested in their 'damned silliness'. Andy noticed an empty treacle-tin – the sort with the little tin neck or spout soldered onto the top for the convenience of pouring out the treacle – and it struck him that this would have made the best kind of cartridge-case: he would only have had to pour in the powder, stick the fuse in through the neck, and cork and seal it with bees-wax. He was turning to suggest this to Dave, when Dave glanced over his shoulder to see how the chops were doing – and bolted. He explained afterwards that he thought he heard the pan spluttering extra, and looked to see if the chops were burning. Jim Bently looked behind and bolted after Dave. Andy stood stock-still, staring after them.

'Run, Andy! Run!' they shouted back at him. 'Run! Look behind you, you fool!' Andy turned slowly and looked, and there close behind him was the retriever with the cartridge in his mouth – wedged into his broadest and silliest grin. And that

wasn't all. The dog had come round the fire to
Andy, and the loose end of the fuse had trailed and
waggled over the burning sticks into the blaze;
Andy had slit and nicked the firing end of the fuse
well, and now it was hissing and spitting properly.

Andy's legs started with a jolt; his legs started
before his brain did, and he made after Dave and
Jim. And the dog followed Andy.

Dave and Jim were good runners – Jim the best –
for a short distance; Andy was slow and heavy, but
he had the strength and the wind and could last. The
dog capered round him, delighted as a dog could be
to find his mates, as he thought, on for a frolic.
Dave and Jim kept shouting back, 'Don't foller us!
Don't foller us, you stupid fool!' But Andy kept on,
no matter how they dodged. They could never
explain, any more than the dog, why they followed
each other, but so they ran, Dave keeping in Jim's
track in all its turnings, Andy after Dave, and the
dog circling round Andy – the live fuse swishing in
all directions and hissing and spluttering and stink-
ing. Jim yelling to Dave not to follow him, Dave
shouting to Andy to go in another direction – to
'spread out', and Andy roaring at the dog to go
home. Then Andy's brain began to work, stimu-
lated by the crisis: he tried to get a running kick at
the dog, but the dog dodged; he snatched up sticks
and stones and threw them at the dog and ran on
again. The retriever saw that he'd made a mistake
about Andy, and left him and bounded after Dave.
Dave, who had the presence of mind to think that
the fuse's time wasn't up yet, made a dive and a

grab for the dog, caught him by the tail, and as he swung round snatched the cartridge out of his mouth and flung it as far as he could; the dog immediately bounded after it and retrieved it. Dave roared and cursed at the dog, who, seeing that Dave was offended, left him and went after Jim, who was well ahead. Jim swung to a sapling and went up it like a native bear; it was a young sapling, and Jim couldn't safely get more than ten or twelve feet from the ground. The dog laid the cartridge, as carefully as if it were a kitten, at the foot of the sapling, and capered and leaped and whooped joyously round under Jim. The big pup reckoned that this was part of the lark – he was all right now – it was Jim who was out for a spree. The fuse sounded as if it were going a mile a minute. Jim tried to climb higher and the sapling bent and cracked. Jim fell on his feet and ran. The dog swooped on the cartridge and followed. It all took but a very few moments. Jim ran to a digger's hole, about ten feet deep, and dropped down into it –

landing on soft mud – and was safe. The dog grinned sardonically down on him, over the edge, for a moment, as if he thought it would be a good lark to drop the cartridge down on Jim.

'Go away, Tommy,' said Jim feebly, 'go away.'

The dog bounded off after Dave, who was the only one in sight now; Andy had dropped behind a log, where he lay flat on his face . . . .

There was a small hotel or shanty on the creek, on the main road, not far from the claim. Dave was desperate, the time flew much faster in his stimu-lated imagination than it did in reality, so he made for the shanty. There were several casual bushmen on the veranda and in the bar; Dave rushed into the bar, banging the door to behind him. 'My dog!' he

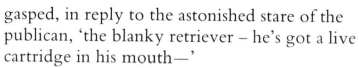

gasped, in reply to the astonished stare of the publican, 'the blanky retriever – he's got a live cartridge in his mouth—'

The retriever, finding the front door shut against him, had bounded round and in by the back way, and now stood smiling in the doorway leading from the passage, the cartridge still in his mouth and the fuse spluttering. They burst out of that bar. Tommy bounded first after one and then after another, for, being a young dog, he tried to make friends with everybody.

The bushmen ran round corners, and some shut themselves in the stable. There was a new weatherboard and corrugated-iron kitchen and wash-house on piles in the backyard, with some women washing clothes inside. Dave and the publican bundled in

41

there and shut the door – the publican cursing Dave and calling him a crimson fool, in hurried tones, and wanting to know what the hell he came here for.

The retriever went in under the kitchen, amongst the piles, but, luckily for those inside, there was a vicious yellow mongrel cattle-dog sulking and nursing his nastiness under there – a sneaking, fighting, thieving canine, whom neighbours had tried for years to shoot or poison. Tommy saw his danger – he'd had experience from this dog – and started out and across the yard, still sticking to the cartridge. Halfway across the yard the yellow dog caught him and nipped him. Tommy dropped the cartridge, gave one terrified yell, and took to the bush. The yellow dog followed him to the fence and then ran back to see what he had dropped. Nearly a dozen other dogs came from round all the corners and under the buildings – spidery, thievish, bold-blooded kangaroo dogs, mongrel sheep- and cattle-dogs, vicious black and yellow dogs – that slip after you in the dark, nip your heels, and vanish without explaining – and yapping, yelping small fry. They kept at a respectable distance round the nasty yellow dog, for it was dangerous to go near him when he thought he had found something which might be good for a dog or cat. He sniffed at the cartridge twice, and was just taking a third cautious sniff when—

It was very good blasting-powder – a new brand that Dave had recently got up from Sydney; and the cartridge had been excellently well made. Andy was very patient and painstaking in all he did, and nearly as handy as the average sailor with needles, twine, canvas and rope. . . .

When the smoke and dust cleared away, the remains of the nasty yellow dog were lying against the paling fence of the yard looking as if he had been kicked into a fire by a horse and afterwards rolled in the dust under a barrow, and finally thrown against the fence from a distance. Several saddle-horses, which had been 'hanging-up' round the veranda, were galloping wildly down the road in clouds of dust, with broken bridle-reins flying; and from a circle round the outskirts, from every point of the compass in the scrub, came the yelping of dogs. Two of them went home, to the place where they were born, thirty miles away, and reached it the same night and stayed there; it was not till towards evening that the rest came back cautiously to make inquiries. One was trying to walk on two legs, and most of 'em looked more or less singed; and a little, singed, stumpy-tailed dog, who had been in the habit of hopping the back half of him along on one leg, had reason to be glad that he'd saved up the other leg all those years, for he needed it now. There was one old one-eyed cattle-dog round that shanty for years afterwards, who couldn't stand the smell of a gun being cleaned. He it was who had taken an interest, only second to that of the yellow dog, in the cartridge. Bushmen said that it was amusing to slip up on his blind side and stick a dirty ramrod under his nose: he wouldn't wait to bring his solitary eye to bear – he'd take to the bush and stay out all night.

For half an hour or so after the explosion there were several bushmen round behind the stable who crouched, doubled up, against the wall, or rolled gently on the dust, trying to laugh without shrieking. There were two white women in hysterics at the house, and a half-caste rushing aimlessly round with a dipper of cold water. The publican was holding his wife tight and begging her between her squawks, to 'hold up for my sake, Mary, or I'll lam the life out of ye.'

Dave decided to apologize later on, 'when things had settled a bit', and went back to camp. And the dog that had done it all, Tommy, the great, idiotic mongrel retriever, came slobbering round Dave and lashing his legs with his tail, and trotted home after him, smiling his broadest, longest, and reddest smile of amiability, and apparently satisfied for one afternoon with the fun he'd had.

Andy chained the dog up securely, and cooked some more chops, while Dave went to help Jim out of the hole.

And most of this is why, for years afterwards, lanky, easy-going bushmen, riding lazily past Dave's camp, would cry, in a lazy drawl and with just a hint of the nasal twang:

''Ello, Da-a-ve! How's the fishin' getting on, Da-a-ve?'

Henry Lawson

My Brother Gets Letters

My brother gets letters – not many, but some,
I don't know why – but I get none.
Odd people seem to write to him –
a card to say his bike's done or a library book's in.
He seems to have friends, who when they're away
write about their holiday,
like – 'We're near the beach, – had chips last night,
my bed squeaks and sand fleas bite.'
And sometimes he gets letters out of the blue
from people who can't know who they're writing to
offering him *The Reader's Digest Bird Book* cheap
or adverts for films like 'The Blobs' – GIANT
     JELLIES THAT EAT AS THEY CREEP.
But I don't get anything. No one writes to me.
That is – until just recently.

You see I was looking at the paper one day
and I was reading about this man's brain – it was
   fading away.
That is – until he had done this 'Memory Course'
and discovered his Inner Mind Force.
And when you got down to the end
It said: 'This sounds GREAT – please send
to me at this address now:
"SO YOU WANT TO SAVE BRAIN-CELLS? – HERE'S
   HOW".'
And you filled in your name and address along
   dotted lines
and sent it off to: 'Great Minds
P.O. Box 16, Manchester 8.'
It was as simple as that. Sit and wait.

Now as it happens I wasn't very worried about my
   Inner Mind Force
or the ones to cure baldness or put me on a
   slimming course,
but the thing was – they all had something for free
which they promised they'd send – addressed to me.
What could be better?
I'd get a letter.
So after I'd got some of these forms together
I came back then to my brother
and I said: 'I bet, out of us two,
I get more letters than you.'
And he said: 'Rubbish, no one ever writes to you,
you're a Nobody, a No-one-knows-who.'
'Right,' I said, 'we'll keep a score,
me and you – see who gets more.'

'Great,' he said, and shook my hand. 'Done!
What do I get,' he said, 'when I've won?'
'No prizes,' I said. 'But whoever loses,
will have to do whatever the winner chooses.'
'Great,' he said again – and laughed,
he must have thought I was daft
to take him on.
He thought he couldn't go wrong.
'I'll show him,' I thought. 'What I can't wait to see
is his face when these people write back to me.'

So anyway, I sent off about three or four
and soon I got what I was hoping for.
A former Mr Universe had written to say:
'BUILD POWER-PACKED MUSCLES
in just 70 seconds a day!!!'
'There you are,' I said to my brother.
'A letter – One nil – and tomorrow I'll be getting
    another.'
So while he read what they had sent me
'Rippling muscles on guarantee
see your strength rise

right before your very eyes
on the built-in POWER-METER,'
I sat tight for my next letter.

Next to come through the post was Harvey Speke.
'I see my years of fatness as a past nightmare I'll
    never repeat.
Why be fat when you can be slim?
Shrink your waistline, stomach and chin,
I used to look like THIS – believe it or not!'
And there were pictures of bellies and heaven knows
    what
before and after shrinking with the Miracle Pill.
I didn't read the rest – 'Two nil!'
I said to my brother. 'I'm winning, aren't I?
You can't win now.' But he says: 'Oh can't I?'
and I can see he's getting really angry
reading about pills to stop you feeling hungry.

Next day there were two more –
one was a rather glossy brochure
on an Old Age Pension Plan
and the other on Shoes For The Larger Man.
For three days he hadn't got anything through the
    post.
He sat there at breakfast munching his toast
staring at his plate while I was making a neat stack
of leaflets and letters I'd got back.
'Four nil now, isn't it? Give in?
You see,' I said, 'every day I'm getting something.'
And sure enough *something* arrived not long after
but it wasn't quite what *I* was after.

It was a great big parcel – it had come from
    Liverpool.
'Who's it for?' I said. 'You, you fool.'
It was the first parcel I'd ever had in my life.
'Go on – open it,' father said, 'here's a knife.'
And they all stood round to see who'd sent a parcel
    to me.
Even my brother wanted to see.

It was wrapped in red paper but the box was brown.
I pulled the lid off – and it was an eiderdown.
'What is it?' 'A pillow?'
'Who sent it?' 'I don't know.'
'How much did it cost you?' 'What do you mean?'
'Don't be funny – he hasn't got a bean.'
I panicked. I came over cold.
Don't forget – I was only nine years old.
'Did you send off for this thing?'
'No,' I said. 'All I did was fill a form thing in,
it said there was something for free –
fill in the form and it'd come to me.'
'Fat-head! That means free till the seventh day,
keep it longer than that and you've got to pay.
Send it back if you don't.
Mind you – I bet you won't.'
'Don't say that,' said mother, 'he wasn't to know
    better.'
'But what was he doing?' 'I wanted a letter.'
'Well get your friend Mart to send you cards from
    Wales when he goes
instead of sending off for boxes of bed-clothes.'

I felt such an idiot looking at the eiderdown.
I looked at my brother. He looked round.
'What's the matter? Five nil. Well done.'
He laughed. 'I think you've won
or do you want to go on for a bit more?'
'No no no,' I said, 'I don't care about the score.'
'So you'll wrap up the box and send it back?' father
    said.
'Unless you want to pay for a new eiderdown on
    your bed.'
But I didn't do it straightaway,
and I didn't do it the next day,
or the next, or the next,
the eiderdown and the wrapping were in a gigantic
    mess.
'The eiderdown's growing,' I was thinking,
'No! The box to send it back in's shrinking.'
Anyway fourth day on – eiderdown still not sent
we were all having tea – the doorbell went.

My brother looks up. 'Probably the police –
on the hunt for an eiderdown thief.'
Father went to see who was there
and we could hear voices from where we were.
Moment later – he's back – very long in the face,
he looks at me. 'It's for you,' he says.
I could have died. 'Is it the police
on the hunt for an eiderdown thief?'
'No,' he says, 'there's a man out there.
He's got something for you.' 'Out where?
Men don't come round here for me.'
But I went to the door and they all followed to see.

'Mr Rosen, is it?' The man looked.
He was reading my name out of a black book.
'No,' I said. 'You want my father.'
'*M.* Rosen?' he says. 'He's *H*, I gather.'
I said, 'Yes. I'm M.'
So he says, 'Good. Right then,
it's outside. Shall I wheel it in?'
'What?' I said. 'The washing machine.'
'Washing machine? Oh no. Not for me.'
'Well it says here "*M.* Rosen", all right. Do you
    want to see?'
'No,' I said, 'I only send for free things.'
'Yes, the demonstrations *are* free,' he says, 'but not
    the washing machines.'
'I don't want it.' I looked round for help.
You can imagine how I felt.
But they were hiding behind the door
laughing their heads off – my brother on the floor.
I turned back. Looked up at the man.
'I've brought it now,' he says. 'It's in the van.'
'I've come all the way from Hoover's to show it
    you.'
'No,' I said. 'No?' he said. 'Haven't you got anyone
    else I could show it to?'
For a moment – it felt like a week –
he looked down at me – I looked down at my feet.
Then he shut his book and went, and I shut the
    door,
and straightaway my brother was there with 'Shall I
    add that to your score?
Six nil? Have you won yet?'
I said, 'I've had enough of this letter bet.'

And he said, 'Why? Don't you want a washing
   machine?
You could use it to keep your eiderdown clean!'
'Oh no! The eiderdown.' For a moment I'd
   forgotten about it.
'I can't get it in. The box: – it's shrunk!' I shouted.
But mum said, 'I'll help you send that back, don't
   worry,
but what's coming next? A coat? A lorry?'
But father said, 'Who's won this bet?
And what's the winner going to get?'
My brother looked really happy and said, 'I've lost –
Letters? *He's* the one that gets the most.'
'All I want,' I said, 'is I don't want to hear any
   more about it.
If I have to send off to get a letter – I'm better off
   without it.'
'OK,' my brother said, 'let's call it square.'
'Yes,' I said, 'we'll leave it there.'

But even now –
when there's someone asking for me at the door,
who mum has never seen before,
she says to me: 'It's for you, dear.
Quick! Your eiderdown's here!'

Michael Rosen

The Gay Goshawk

The horse walked under the great beeches, lazily padding by the side of the road. Now and again he stopped to graze, his white head cropping the grass, his tail sweeping the flies away in slow rhythmic switches. Always, after he had eaten, he went on again in the same direction, along the road which led to his stable.

The knight sat with his head drooping, one hand listless on the reins. The wound in his stomach had almost stopped bleeding now, but he could feel its edges pouting like a red mouth. There was no pain, no sensation, but his face was pinched with past agony, the lips and eyes blue shadowed. At last, so quietly, so easily that he hardly realized it, he leaned farther forward, drooped sideways, and slid to the ground. His horse gazed at him sadly, mildly, and went on. Now he lay under a green hedge, with the grasses sweeping his face, and a nettle grinning at him with green teeth. The sky darkened and spun as the pain returned, and his face grew cold in the sunshine.

The horse went on under the beeches, his silken ornaments tawdry and draggled. There was no one to stop him, to question or harass him with farther journeyings and loud frightened cries. The castle gate swung open, wide and untended, and, unseen, he padded the dusty path, and stopped to graze where the grass was greenest.

They had left the castle two days ago, when they heard that the enemy were coming. A shrill scream had run over the countryside, a cry of alarm, and the women had listened with pale faces. 'The enemy! The enemy! Our men are fighting, but they cannot hold them! Give them the castle, give them our homes, our riches, our land – it is easier to part with these than with our honour!' There had been dark rumours, murmured among the matrons. Not only the young, but the old, the mothers and grandmothers, had been used . . . they filled their hands, they grabbed what they could, and, in an hour, the stables were emptied, and the lady of the castle headed the retreat, her robes flowing, her hands grasping the reins like a man's, beating out the words, 'Oh, hurry! Hurry!'

Now they were far away, in hiding, waiting for news. They clung together, afraid of what they might hear, and their conscience goaded them to self-justification. 'What could we have done? Our knives against their swords, our spades against their battle-axes . . . and they are warriors, well used to fighting! We should have been dragged out, trampled underfoot – best for us to escape with our lives!'

The castle was deserted, inside and out. The battlements jutted sharp into the sky, the flag drooped on its pole. In the kitchen, a yellow dog whined and stretched itself before the hearth. The big black pot was bedded in ashes, and the soup inside had turned sour, a rancid scum mottling the surface, a thin dust sifted over it from the shifting of the fire. Long yellow streaks showed where the broth had boiled over, cooled and congealed. The pitchers of milk on the table had also soured and set, and the bread on the platter was hard as a rock; but the dog's water dish was dry, and the bone he had been gnawing was now white and smooth, kicked into the corner by a hasty foot.

The dog was thirsty. The vermin which trespassed at night had kept him from hunger, but there was no water anywhere. Yawning, his eyes dull, he stretched himself and set off on another search. He could not understand the silence. He thirsted for company even more than for drink. If a man had entered the kitchen, the dog would have leaped on him and overturned him in ecstatic welcome.

Slowly, he nosed around, whining, a high singing

plaint. The scrubbed tables and ledges were out of his reach. He reared on his hind legs, paws resting, head craning, but there was nothing to drink, not even a splash of water carelessly spilt. Quietly, patiently, he pattered out, his claws scratching bluntly, his head poked forward in the dust of the passages. Even the cat had gone. He pushed against a door which stood ajar, and found himself in the high dining hall. From habit, he went to his old corner beside the hearth, where he would wait for his master to throw him the bones and scraps from his plate. Head erect, ears cocked he waited, but there was no one in the high chair, no sound of laughter, no red faces flaming over the wine-flagon. He sighed, and his ears drooped, and his tail went limp between his legs.

He could smell his master's presence, faint in the air. He could smell the scents of women, puzzling, elusive. Where had they gone, the men who spoke roughly and laughed, the women who fondled his ears and kissed his yellow head? Up the stairs he went, round and round, up and up, like a dog on a treadmill. Here, there were rooms which told the story of flight. He poked his head into every one, but backed out again, timid, defeated.

In the last room, the largest, something was stirring, a flurry of sound, a soft metallic jingle. He tiptoed in, whimpering. A velvet gown was thrown on the floor with satin slippers and a box of bright silks. The couch where my lady had lain was all in disorder, and her brushes lay askew on the table. On a perch by the window, a goshawk rustled its

striped feathers, and stamped angrily, trying to jerk
itself free. It looked at the dog, and the dog leaped
forward, yelping and panting and wagging his tail
frantically.

The bird sat still, quieted for the moment. The
velvet on the floor was ruffled under the dog's feet,
and the slippers and trinkets were scattered as he
pranced in joy. Yap! Yap! he went, and the noise of
his breathing filled the pauses between his barks.
The bird's head crouched lower and lower, till at
last it lunged forward with its wings raised and its
beak hooked and vicious. It stabbed twice, and the
dog rolled back in dismay, still yelping, and hurt at
the unexpected hostility. Once again, he tripped up
to the perch, his eyes pleading, but the goshawk
glared and beat at him, rattling its fine silver chain,
so that he retreated howling, down the stone stairs
to the quiet and the loneliness.

The white horse stood before his stables in his
torn trappings. Inside was food and shade from the
sun, but the door was shut, and no friendly hand
came to open it. Everything was dusty and dry, no
water anywhere. The fountain in the yard had
stopped playing long ago, and though one of the
pipes still trickled, it left only a thick smear of slime,
oozing over the stone basin. The horse snuffed at it,
and turned away. The sun was very hot, and a bad
smell came from the green–coated stone. Patiently,
his harness heavy, he waited by the stable, and
switched the flies away.

The dog heard the scrape of hooves, and whined
at every cranny, every slit where the stone was worn

under the oaken doors. He fawned and grovelled,
almost insane with longing, and the horse turned
mildly and jingled his bridle. At last, the yapping
died to a whimper, and faded, as the dog lay with
his head on its paws and slept exhausted.

Up in the tower, the goshawk stared coldly at the
tumbled finery of my lady's boudoir, and wrenched
afresh at its chain.

The knight lay with his knees drawn up to ease
the gash in his stomach. His mouth was dry, and
though he could feel the stones sharp under him, he

had no strength to move. He could not even lift a hand to wipe the dust from his face.

Where was he? The world was all out of focus. There was a rustle of leaves over his head, and grasses waved round him, tickling his ears with their feathery tips. His heel, when he moved it, grated on grit, but he could not puzzle out where he was lying, or which way the road went. When had he come here? Where was his horse? He remembered his wound and the desperate retreat; he remembered being alone, letting the horse take his own way; but after that, there was nothing.

The sky was a deep blue, shading off pale towards the horizon. Against the blueness, the leaves over-head were black, and the grass in which he lay was colourless. It must be night. The moon had not yet risen, but when he tried to calculate the time, his head swam, and he could not think. He lay quiet, almost content, full of a childlike pleasure in being able to stare at the blueness without blinking.

There was no wind, and yet the beech leaves, infinitely more remote than the sky, rustled and trembled miles up in space. The nettle which had grinned in daylight now stood like a spiky sentinel, every leaf rigid and strong. It was too virile, too tense among the delicate grasses. He looked back to the sky, from the farthest turquoise edge to the deep azure above; and then he turned his head and saw the battlemented edge of his castle against the deepest blue of all, and the world swung into focus so suddenly that it dizzied him, and he clung to the ground for safety, forgetting that he could not fall.

60

His home was just beyond the opposite hedge. A little farther on were the gates, and then the drive curving back in shadow till it reached the castle. His horse must have gone on alone. Why, then, had nobody come to help him? Perhaps they had not guessed he could be so near. Perhaps the horse had gone back to his stable unseen. They were often idle, these hostlers, and, knowing their master to be away, they would be neglecting their duties. Well, any time now, they would come for him. . . .

With an effort, he dug his hands into the grass and levered himself higher, leaning against the bank. Strange how weak his arms were! He felt the wound drag its crusted edges, and drew up his legs again. Now he could watch the tower, and wait for them coming. They would bring lights, and a litter to carry him home. They would have water, and the unguents to salve his wound, wine for his parched throat, and soft linen to lie on. And his lady would weep over him, but smile because he had returned to her.

It was very quiet, as still as death. No voices carried from the castle, no lights winked from the windows. An owl swept past, like a shadow, and a faint glitter of stars was washed up on the deepening tide of blue.

Next time he woke, he thought that day had come. The sky had lightened, and the moon was so bright that he could see everything, the stones in the road, the blood on his clothes, and the colour of the bluebells in the grass, pale beside the crimson of clover. The dead white light poured down, and he

was suddenly afraid. Why did they not come? Did
his lady not feel, did she not sense that he was here?
He turned his head restlessly, but he could not move
himself more. It was like lying in a nightmare,
pressed down by the knotted covers and the weight
of sleep. His head was giddy with too much moon-
light. Perhaps he was sleeping now. He would be
better in the morning. The dream would pass, and
he would rise up rested, and walk into the great
hall, and they would flock to welcome him, and *she*
would nurse him back to his old strength.

He started. His dog, his little yellow dog, was
howling! Far away, it lifted its head and howled at
the moon, a long bay dying away in sorrow. The
knight was weak, and the sound made the sweat
start all over his body. 'Hey, Jako!' he tried to call,
but the voice stuck in his throat, and his lips were
too dry to whistle. When the howling had died
away, he watched the tower, ready for all manner of
curses to fall on it, witches skimming the coping like
bats, flames leaping red from the stone, but the
moon shone steady and pale, and nothing moved,
not even the dust.

He opened his eyes again, not knowing that he
had slept. His head was heavy, the whole world
pressing down on him, and his mouth was dry,
burned up with fever. The sky was grey, the grasses
moist and fresh, and the castle seemed far away now,
happed in a white mist. It was cold, so cold that
there was hardly any sense in his limbs. It took him
a long time to think, to remember who and where
he was, and why he was lying in damp grass with

nothing to moisten his lips or slake his throat. His mind went wandering in circles, like the bird which hovered above him, round and round, never settling, but never leaving the one spot. . . .

He started when it alighted beside him, pleased at its nearness, the tameness which let it stand unafraid. Idly, he watched its eyes, its strong beak and barred feathers. It was a beautiful bird. . . .

His mind was so slow that, at first, the chain on its leg meant nothing to him. It was a delicate chain, broken off raggedly, and round the leg was a silver ring, the coat of arms graven finely, so that it stood out clear for all it was so minute. When at last the meaning seeped into him, a faint flush of warmth ran into his body. Strength came back to his hands and his fingers fretted and tore at the torn silk of his cloak, but all he could wrench off was one thread. He held out his arm, and the bird came nearer, as it was used to do when he called. Fumbling with weakness, he looped the stuff inside the looseness of the ring, till the bird protested and flapped its wings. It was done, though. It was accomplished. Now, as it had been taught, it would fly to its mistress, and soon, soon. . . .

It would not move. Sinister, it raked its beak along its claws, and ruffled its soft feathers. Its eyes were cold, but expectant. And suddenly, the knight knew that there was no one for it to fly to, and that it would watch beside him now till the last. Beyond that, he did not care to think.

Dorothy K. Haynes

The Giant and the Man

It is like this: A man is going fishing because he is
hungry. He is fishing, but he still hasn't caught any.
He is fishing for a long time now, looking about in
all directions for game. He is still fishing. Because he
is looking, turning his head about in all directions
for anything, he sees a man who is coming over the
horizon and who is overly large. He sees a giant and
is wondering what to do. 'I'm going to be killed,' he
thinks. Having heard that giants are usually alone,
he thinks, 'Perhaps I will pretend to be dead.' And
so he pretends to be dead. As the giant is arriving, he
holds his breath. When he arrives, the giant is
listening to see whether he has any breath. As he has
no breath, he takes hold of him. 'He has no
strength and so he is dead,' the giant thinks. So then
he seizes him, wishing to carry him on the back
with a line. He ties him up for carrying. The man is
pretending to be frozen and tries not to breathe. He
makes a lot of effort not to breathe at all as he is
being carried on the back. He looks frozen since he
is pretending to be so. He sees willows as they were
going through them. While the man is being
carried, he gets an idea, 'Now maybe if I grabbed
onto the willows, he will get tired.'
  He has been grabbing onto the bushes and letting
go of them, and the giant has been pulling hard.
When, after taking hold of the bushes, he releases
them, the giant nearly falls down. When he nearly

falls over, the giant rests, listening for breath but with the man appearing not to have any. Starting to walk again, he goes through the willows. When the man, grabbing the willows, pulls hard, the giant almost falls down. He is tiring, the giant, because the man has been pulling hard.

He reaches his big home. The giant carries the man in and props him up by the entrance. Since he is too tired to want to do anything at all, he lies down on the sleeping platform. His big wife is gone to get some wood, the man being the reason for getting the wood. When the man knows that he is the reason for gathering wood, he opens the corners of his eyes just a tiny bit. He is trying to look around a little while seeming not to look for anything. The big children say, 'Father, his eyes are opening.' The giant answers, 'That one down there hasn't any breath; he's dead.'

The man notices the giant's big axe beside him because he feels it. The giant is going to sleep. Although he is being spoken to by his big children, he no longer answers. When the man thinks he is asleep, he takes the axe while appearing not to. He axes the giant. While the big entrance, which can be pinned shut, is still open, he goes out.

Going out, he sees the big wife. The man runs away. Seeing him, the big woman has started to chase him, and is gaining on him. When the man is almost overtaken, he has an idea: 'Maybe if I chop it, it will split apart,' he thinks. So he chops and a river flows. The man goes on the other side. He waits, trying to find out what will happen.

The big woman is stopping and saying,
  'How did you get across this?'
  'By drinking it,' she is answered.
  So then, the big woman starts drinking. When
she is about to burst, she is told by the man, 'Finish
it now.' And so, trying to finish it, she is drinking
extremely fast. She simply bursts, exploding. When
she bursts, she forms mist. It's very foggy all around.
This is how fog came to be everywhere. The man
just stayed put there because it was foggy and he
didn't know where to go. When it became windy,
the fog was blown away, and when the fog was
gone, he started home. These then are the words
about 'The Giant and the Man'.

Traditional Eskimo story

In the Daytime

In the daytime I am Rob Roy and a tiger
In the daytime I am Marco Polo
          I chase bears in Bricket Wood
In the daytime I am the Tower of London
          nothing gets past me
          when it's my turn
          in Harrybo's hedge
In the daytime I am Henry the fifth and Ulysses
          and I tell stories
          that go on for a whole week
          if I want.
At night in the dark
          when I've shut the front room door
          I try and
          get up the stairs across the landing
          into bed and under the pillow
          without breathing once.

Michael Rosen

Small Singing

Small's singing was joyful noise more than music;
what it lacked in elegance it made up in volume. As
fire cannot help giving heat so Small's happiness
could not help giving song, in spite of family
complaint. They called her singing a 'horrible row',
and said it shamed them before the neighbours, but
Small sang on. She sang in the cow-yard, mostly,
not that she went there specially to sing, but she was
so happy when she was there among the creatures
that the singing did itself. She had but to open her
mouth and the noise jumped out.

The moment Small sat down upon the cow-yard
woodpile the big rooster would jump into her lap
and the cow amble across the yard to plant her
squareness, one leg under each corner, right in front
of Small, and to shut out completely the view of the
old red barn, the hen houses, and the manure-pile.

The straight outline of the cow's back in front of
Small was like a range of mountains with low hills
and little valleys. The tail end of the cow was as
square as a box. Horns were her only curve – back,
front, tail, neck and nose in profile, were all straight
lines. Even the slobber dripping from her chin fell in
slithery streaks.

When Small began to sing, the old cow's nose-
line shot from straight down to straight out, her
chin rose into the air, her jaws rolled. The harder
Small sang, the harder the cow chewed and the

faster she twiddled her ears around as if stirring the song into the food to be rechewed in cud along with her breakfast.

Small loved her cow-yard audience – hens twisting their silly heads and clawing the earth with mincing feet, their down eye looking for grubs, their up eye peering at Small, ducks trying hard to out-quack the song, pigeons clapping their white wings, rabbits hoisting and sinking their noses – whether in appreciation or derision Small could never tell.

White fluttered through the cow-yard gate, Bigger's apron heralding an agitated Bigger, both hands wrestling with the buttons of her apron behind and her tongue ready sharpened to attack Small's singing.

'It's disgusting! Stop that vulgar row, Small! What must the neighbours think? Stop it, I say!'

Small sang harder, bellowing the words, 'The cow likes it and this is her yard.'

'I wish to goodness that she would roof her yard then, or that you would sing under an umbrella, Small, and so keep the sound down and not let it boil over the fences. There's the breakfast bell! Throw that fowl out of your lap and come! Song before breakfast means tears before night.'

'Whose tears – mine, the cow's or the rooster's?'

'Oh, oh, oh! That cow-brute has dripped slobber down my clean apron! You're a disgusting pair,' shrieked Bigger and rushed from the yard.

Breakfast over, the Elder detained Small.

'Small, this singing of yours is scandalous! Yesterday I was walking up the street with a lady. Half a block from our gate she stopped dead. "Listen! Someone is in trouble," she said. How do you think I felt saying, "Oh, no, it is only my little sister singing"?'

Small reddened but said stubbornly. 'The cow likes my singing.'

Cows are different from humans; perhaps the hairiness of their ears strains sound.

The Bishop came to pay a sick-visit to Small's mother. He prayed and Small watched and listened.

His deliberate chewing of the words, with closed eyes, reminded her of the cow chewing her cud. The Bishop was squarely built, a slow calm man. 'They are very alike,' thought Small.

Rising from his knees, the Bishop, aware of the little girl's stare, said, 'You grow, child!'

'She does,' said Small's mother. 'So does her voice; her singing is rather a family problem.'

'Song is good,' replied Bishop. 'Is it hymns you sing, child?'

'No, Mr Bishop. I prefer cow-songs.'

The Bishop's 'a-a-h!' long drawn and flat lasted all the way down the stairs.

'You should not have said that,' said Small's mother. 'A Bishop is a Bishop.'

'And a cow is a cow. Is it so wicked to sing to a cow?'

'Not wicked at all. I love your happy cow-yard songs coming into my window. We will have your voice trained some day. Then perhaps the others will not scold so much about your singing.'

'But will the cow like my voice squeezed little and polite? It won't be half so much fun singing beautifully as boiling over like the jam kettle.'

Emily Carr

Assignment with an Octopus

The fear I had for the larger kinds of octopus was a blind fear, sick with disgust, unreasoned as a child's horror of darkness. Victor Hugo was the man who first brought it up to the level of my conscious thought. I still remember vividly the impression left on me as a boy of fourteen by that account in *Les Travailleurs de la Mer* of Gilliatt's fight with the monster that caught him among the rocks of The Douvres. For years after reading it, I tortured myself with wondering how ever I could behave with decent courage if faced with a giant at once so strong and so loathsome. My commonest nightmare of the period was of an octopus-like Presence poised motionless behind me, towards which I dared not turn, from which my limbs were too frozen to escape. But that phase did pass before I left school, and the Thing lay dormant inside me until a day at Tarawa.

Before I reached Tarawa, however, chance gave me a swift glimpse of what a biggish octopus could do to a man. I was wading at low tide one calm evening on the lip of the reef at Ocean Island when a Baanaban villager, back from fishing, brought his canoe to land within twenty yards of where I stood. There was no more than a show of breaking seas, but the water was only knee deep, and this obliged the fisherman to slide overboard and handle his lightened craft over the jagged edge. But no sooner were his feet upon the reef than he seemed to be

tied to where he stood. The canoe was washed
shorewards ahead of him, while he stood with legs
braced, tugging desperately away from something.
I had just time to see a tapering, greyish-yellow rope
curled around his right wrist before he broke away
from it. He fell sprawling into the shallow water;
the tapered rope flicked writhing back into the foam
at the reef's edge. The fisherman picked himself up
and nursed his right arm. I had reached him by then.
The octopus had caught him with only the tip of
one tentacle, but the terrible hold of the few suckers
on his wrist had torn the skin whole from it as he
wrenched himself adrift.

This is not to say that all the varieties of octopus known to the Gilbertese are dangerous to man. Some of them are mere midgets, and very beautiful. Lying face down on a canoe anchored over rocks and sand in Tarawa lagoon, I sometimes used to watch for the smaller kinds through a water-glass.

The smallest I saw could have been comfortably spread on the lid of a cigarette tin. I noticed that the colours of all the little ones varied very much according to where they were crawling, from the mottled rust-red and brown of coral rock to the clear gold and orange-brown of sunlit sand speckled with seaweed. From the height of my top-window, most of them looked as flat as starfish slithering over the bottom, but there was one minute creature that had a habit of standing on its toes. It would constrict its tentacles into a kind of neck where they joined the head and, with its body so raised, would jig up and down rather like a dancing frog. But what appealed most to my wonder was the way they all swam. A dozen sprawling, lace-like shapes would suddenly gather themselves into streamlines and shoot upwards, jet-propelled by the marvellous syphon in their heads, like a display of fairy water-rockets. At the top of their flight, they seemed to explode; their tails of trailed tentacles burst outwards into shimmering points around their tiny bodies, and they sank like drifting gossamer stars back to the sea-floor again.

The female octopus anchors her eggs to stalks of weed and coral under water. It seems to be a moot point whether she broods in their neighbourhood or not, but I once saw what I took to be a mother out for exercise with five babies. She had a body about the size of a tennis ball and tentacles perhaps a foot long. The length of the small ones, streamlined for swimming, was not more than five inches over all. They were cruising around a coral pinnacle in four feet of water. The big one led, the babies followed six inches behind, in what seemed to be an ordered formation: they were grouped, as it were, around the base of a cone whereof she was the forward-pointing apex.

They cruised around the pinnacle for half a minute or more, and then went down to some small rocks at its base. While the little ones sprawled over the bottom, the mother remained poised above them. It looked to my inexpert eye exactly as if she was mounting guard over her young. And at that point a big trevally was obliging enough to become the villain of a family drama for my benefit. He must have been watching the little group from deeper water. As the mother hovered there, he came in at her like a blue streak. But she avoided him somehow; he flashed by and turned to dart in again, only to see a black cloud of squirted ink where the octopus had been. (Incidentally, that was the only time I myself ever saw an octopus discharge its inksac.) The trevally swerved aside, fetched a full circle and came very slowly back to the edge of the black cloud, while the mother and her family were escaping towards the shallows on the other side. He loitered around for a while, then seemed to take fright and flicked away at speed into the deep water.

The old navigators of the Gilberts used to talk with fear of a gigantic octopus that inhabited the seas between Samoa and the Ellice Islands. They said its tentacles were three arm-spans long and thicker at the base than the body of a full-grown man – a scale of measurements not out of keeping with what is known of the atrocious monster called *Octopus Apollyon*. There were some who stated that this foul fiend of the ocean was also to be found in the waters between Onotoa, Tamana and Aroae in the Southern Gilberts. But I never came across a man who had seen one, and the biggest of the octopus breed I ever saw with my own eyes had tentacles only a little over six feet long. It was a member of the clan *Octopus Vulgaris*, which swarms in all the lagoons. An average specimen of this variety is a dwarf beside *Octopus Apollyon*: laid out flat, it has a total spread of no more than nine or ten feet; but it is a wicked-looking piece of work, even in death, with those disgusting suckers studding its arms and those bulging, filmed eyes staring out of the mottled gorgon face.

Possibly, if you can watch objectively, the sight of *Octopus Vulgaris* searching for crabs and crayfish on the floor of the lagoon may move you to something like admiration. You cannot usually see the dreadful eyes from a water-glass straight above its feeding-ground, and your feeling for crustaceans is too impersonal for horror at their fate between pouncing suckers and jaws. There is real beauty in the rich change of its colours as it moves from shadow to sunlight, and the gliding ease of its arms as they reach and flicker over the rough rocks fascinates the eye with its deadly grace. You feel that if only the creature would stick to its grubbing on the bottom, the shocking ugliness of its shape might even win your sympathy, as for some poor Caliban in the enchanted garden of the lagoon. But it is no honest grubber in the open. For every one of its kind that you see crawling below you, there are a dozen skulking in recesses of the reef that falls away like a cliff from the edge where you stand watching. When *Octopus Vulgaris* has eaten its fill of the teeming crabs and crayfish, it seeks a dark cleft in the coral face, and anchors itself there with a few of the large suckers nearest to its body. Thus shielded from attack in the rear, with tentacles gathered to pounce, it squats glaring from the shadows, alert for anything alive to swim within striking distance. It can hurl one or all of those whiplashes forward with the speed of dark lightning, and once its scores of

suckers, rimmed with hooks for grip on slippery skins, are clamped about their prey, nothing but the brute's death will break their awful hold.

But that very quality of the octopus that most horrifies the imagination, its relentless tenacity, becomes its undoing when hungry man steps into the picture. The Gilbertese happen to value certain parts of it as food, and their method of fighting it is coolly based upon the one fact that its arms never change their grip. They hunt for it in pairs. One man acts as the bait, his partner as the killer. First, they swim eyes-under at low tide just off the reef, and search the crannies of the submarine cliff for sight of any tentacle that may flicker out for a catch. When they have placed their quarry, they land on the reef for the next stage. The human bait starts the real game. He dives and tempts the lurking brute by swimming a few strokes in front of its cranny, at first a little beyond striking range. Then he turns and makes straight for the cranny, to give himself into the embrace of those waiting arms. Sometimes nothing happens. The beast will not always respond to the lure. But usually it strikes.

The partner on the reef above stares down through the pellucid water, waiting for his moment. His teeth are his only weapon. His killing efficiency depends on his avoiding every one of those strangling arms. He must wait until his partner's body has been drawn right up to the entrance of the cleft. The monster inside is groping then with its horny mouth against the victim's flesh, and sees nothing beyond it. That point is reached in a matter of no more than thirty seconds after the decoy has plunged. The killer dives, lays hold of his pinioned friend at arms' length, and jerks him away from the cleft; the octopus is torn adrift from the anchorage of its proximal suckers, and clamps itself the more fiercely to its prey. In the same second, the human bait gives a kick which brings him, with quarry annexed, to the surface. He turns on his back, still holding his breath for better buoyancy, and this exposes the body of the beast for the kill. The killer closes in, grasps the evil head from behind, and wrenches it away from its meal. Turning the face up towards himself, he plunges his teeth between the bulging eyes, and bites down and in with all his strength. That is the end of it. It dies on the instant; the suckers release their hold; the arms fall away; the two fishers paddle with whoops of delighted laughter to the reef, where they string the catch to a pole before going to rout the next one.

Any two boys of seventeen, any day of the week, will go out and get you half a dozen octopus like that for the mere fun of it. Here lies the whole point of this story. The hunt is, in the most literal sense, nothing but child's play to the Gilbertese.

As I was standing one day at the end of a jetty in Tarawa lagoon, I saw two boys from the near village shouldering a string of octopus slung on a pole between them. I started to wade out in their direction, but before I hailed them they had stopped, planted the carrying-pole upright in a fissure and, leaving it there, swum off the edge for a while with faces submerged, evidently searching for something

under water. I had been only a few months at
Tarawa, and that was my first near view of an
octopus-hunt. I watched every stage of it from the
dive of the human bait to the landing of the dead
catch. When it was over, I went up to them. I could
hardly believe that in those few seconds, with no
more than a frivolous-looking splash or two on the
surface, they could have found, caught and killed
the creature they were now stringing up before my
eyes. They explained the amusing simplicity of the
thing.

'There's only one trick the decoy-man must never
forget,' they said, 'and that's not difficult to
remember. If he is not wearing the water-spectacles
of the Men of Matang, he must cover his eyes with a
hand as he comes close to the *kika* (octopus), or the
suckers might blind him.' It appeared that the
ultimate fate of the eyes was not the thing to worry
about; the immediate point was that the sudden
pain of a sucker clamping itself to an eyeball might
cause the bait to expel his breath and inhale sea-
water; that would spoil his buoyancy, and he would
fail then to give his friend the best chance of a kill.

Then they began whispering together. I knew in a
curdling flash what they were saying to each other.
Before they turned to speak to me again, a horrified
conviction was upon me. My damnable curiosity
had led me into a trap from which there was no
escape. They were going to propose that I should
take a turn at being the bait myself, just to see how
delightfully easy it was. And that is what they did.
It did not even occur to them that I might not leap

82

at the offer. I was already known as a young Man of Matang who liked swimming, and fishing, and laughing with the villagers; I had just shown an interest in this particular form of hunting; naturally, I should enjoy the fun of it as much as they did. Without even waiting for my answer, they gleefully ducked off the edge of the reef to look for another octopus – a fine fat one – *mine*. Left standing there alone, I had another of those visions. . . .

It was dusk in the village. The fishers were home, I saw the cooking-fires glowing orange-red between the brown lodges. There was laughter and shouted talk as the women prepared the evening meal. But the laughter was hard with scorn. 'What?' they were saying. 'Afraid of a *kika*? The young Man of Matang? Why, even our boys are not afraid of a *kika*!' A curtain went down and rose again on the Residency; the Old Man was talking: 'A leader? You? The man who funked a schoolboy game? We don't leave your sort in charge of Districts.' The scene flashed to my uncles: 'Returned empty,' they said. 'We always knew you hadn't got it in you. Returned empty. . . .'

Of course it was all overdrawn, but one fact was beyond doubt: the Gilbertese reserved all their most ribald humour for physical cowardice. No man gets himself passed for a leader anywhere by becoming the butt of that kind of wit. I decided I would rather face the octopus.

I was dressed in khaki slacks, canvas shoes and a short-sleeved singlet. I took off the shoes and made up my mind to shed the singlet if told to do so; but

83

I was wildly determined to stick to my trousers throughout. Dead or alive, said a voice within me, an official minus his pants is a preposterous object, and I felt I could not face that extra horror. However, nobody asked me to remove anything.

I hope I did not look as yellow as I felt when I stood to take the plunge; I have never been so sick with funk before or since. 'Remember, one hand for your eyes,' said someone from a thousand miles off, and I dived.

I do not suppose it is really true that the eyes of an octopus shine in the dark; besides, it was clear daylight only six feet down in the limpid water; but I could have sworn the brute's eyes burned at me as I turned in towards his cranny. That dark glow – whatever may have been its origin – was the last thing I saw as I blacked out with my left hand and rose into his clutches. Then, I remember chiefly a dreadful sliminess with a herculean power behind it. Something whipped round my left forearm and the back of my neck, binding the two together. In the same flash, another something slapped itself high on my forehead, and I felt it crawling down inside the back of my singlet. My impulse was to tear at it with my right hand, but I felt the whole of that arm pinioned to my ribs. In most emergencies the mind works with crystal-clear impersonality. This was not even an emergency, for I knew myself perfectly safe. But my boyhood's nightmare was upon me. When I felt the swift constriction of those disgusting arms jerk my head and shoulders in towards the reef, my mind went blank of every thought save the beastliness of contact with that squat head. A mouth began to nuzzle below my throat, at the junction of the collar-bones. I forgot there was anyone to save me. Yet something still directed me to hold my breath.

I was awakened from my cowardly trance by a quick, strong pull on my shoulders, back from the cranny. The cables around me tightened painfully, but I knew I was adrift from the reef. I gave a kick, rose to the surface and turned on my back with the brute sticking out of my chest like a tumour. My mouth was smothered by some flabby moving horror. The suckers felt like hot rings pulling at my skin. It was only two seconds, I suppose, from then to the attack of my deliverer, but it seemed like a century of nausea.

My friend came up between me and the reef. He pounced, pulled, bit down, and the thing was over – for everyone but me. At the sudden relaxation of the tentacles, I let out a great breath, sank, and drew in the next under water. It took the united help of both boys to get me, coughing, heaving and pretending to join in their delighted laughter, back to the reef. I had to submit there to a kind of war-dance round me, in which the dead beast was slung whizzing past my head from one to the other. I had a chance to observe then that it was not by any stretch of fancy a giant, but just plain average. That took the bulge out of my budding self-esteem. I left hurriedly for the cover of the jetty, and was sick.

Arthur Grimble

A Perfect Liar

Once upon a time there was a King of Armenia, who, being of a curious turn of mind and in need of some new diversion, sent his heralds throughout the land to make the following proclamation:

'Hear this! Whatever man among you can prove himself the most outrageous liar in Armenia shall receive an apple made of pure gold from the hands of His Majesty the King!'

People began to swarm to the palace from every town and hamlet in the country, people of all ranks and conditions, princes, merchants, farmers, priests, rich and poor, tall and short, fat and thin. There was no lack of liars in the land, and each one told his tale to the King. A ruler, however, has heard practically every sort of lie, and none of those now told him convinced the King that he had listened to the best of them.

The King was beginning to grow tired of his new sport and was thinking of calling the whole contest off without declaring a winner, when there appeared before him a poor, ragged man, carrying a large earthenware pitcher under his arm.

'What can I do for you?' asked His Majesty.

'Sire!' said the poor man, slightly bewildered. 'Surely you remember? You owe me a pot of gold, and I have come to collect it.'

'You are a perfect liar, sir!' exclaimed the King. 'I owe you no money!'

'A perfect liar, am I?' said the poor man. 'Then give me the golden apple!'

The King, realizing that the man was trying to trick him, started to hedge.

'No, no! You are not a liar!'

'Then give me the pot of gold you owe me, Sire,' said the man.

The King saw the dilemma. He handed over the golden apple.

Armenian folk tale

The Golden Kite, the Silver Wind

'In the shape of a *pig*?' cried the Mandarin.

'In the shape of a pig,' said the messenger, and departed.

'Oh, what an evil day in an evil year,' cried the Mandarin. 'The town of Kwan-Si, beyond the hill, was very small in my childhood. Now it has grown so large that at last they are building a wall.'

'But why should a wall two miles away make my good father sad and angry all within the hour?' asked his daughter quietly.

'They build their wall,' said the Mandarin, 'in the shape of a pig! Do you see? Our own city wall is built in the shape of an orange. That pig will devour us, greedily!'

'Ah.'

They both sat thinking.

Life was full of symbols and omens. Demons lurked everywhere, Death swam in the wetness of an eye, the turn of a gull's wing meant rain, a fan held *so*, the tilt of a roof, and, yes, even a city wall was of immense importance. Travellers and tourists, caravans, musicians, artists, coming upon these two towns, equally judging the portents, would say, 'The city shaped like an orange? No! I will enter the city shaped like a pig and prosper, eating all, growing fat with good luck and prosperity!'

The Mandarin wept. 'All is lost! These symbols and signs terrify. Our city will come on evil days.'

'Then,' said the daughter, 'call in your stonemasons and temple builders, I will whisper from
behind the silken screen and you will know the
words.'

The old man clapped his hands despairingly. 'Ho,
stonemasons! Ho, builders of towns and palaces!'

The men who knew marble and granite and onyx
and quartz came quickly. The Mandarin faced them
most uneasily, himself waiting for a whisper from
the silken screen behind his throne. At last the
whisper came.

'I have called you here,' said the whisper.

'I have called you here,' said the Mandarin aloud, 'because our city is shaped like an orange, and the vile city of Kwan-Si has this day shaped theirs like a ravenous pig—'

The stonemasons groaned and wept. Death rattled his cane in the outer courtyard. Poverty made a sound like a wet cough in the shadows of the room.

'And so,' said the whisper, said the Mandarin, 'you raisers of walls must go bearing trowels and rocks and change the shape of *our* city!'

The architects and masons gasped. The Mandarin himself gasped at what he had said. The whisper whispered. The Mandarin went on: 'And you will change our walls into a club which may beat the pig and drive it off!'

The stonemasons rose up, shouting. Even the Mandarin, delighted at the words from his mouth, applauded, stood down from his throne. 'Quick!' he cried. 'To work!'

When his men had gone, smiling and bustling, the Mandarin turned with great love to the silken screen. 'Daughter,' he whispered, 'I will embrace you.' There was no reply. He stepped around the screen, and she was gone.

Such modesty, he thought. She has slipped away and left me with a triumph, as if it were mine.

The news spread through the city; the Mandarin was acclaimed. Everyone carried stone to the walls. Fireworks were set off and the demons of death and poverty did not linger, as all worked together. At the end of the month the wall had been changed. It was now a mighty bludgeon with which to drive pigs, boars, even lions, far away. The Mandarin slept like a happy fox every night.

'I would like to see the Mandarin of Kwan-Si when the news is learned. Such pandemonium and hysteria; he will likely throw himself from a mountain! A little more of that wine, oh Daughter-who-thinks-like-a-son.'

But the pleasure was like a winter flower; it died swiftly. That very afternoon the messenger rushed into the courtroom. 'Oh, Mandarin, disease, early sorrow, avalanches, grasshopper plagues, and poisoned well water!'

The Mandarin trembled.

'The town of Kwan-Si,' said the messenger, 'which was built like a pig and which animal we drove away by changing our walls to a mighty stick, has now turned triumph to winter ashes. They have built their city's walls like a great bonfire to burn our stick!'

The Mandarin's heart sickened within him, like an autumn fruit upon an ancient tree. 'Oh, gods! Travellers will spurn us. Tradesmen, reading the symbols, will turn from the stick, so easily destroyed, to the fire, which conquers all!'

'No,' said a whisper like a snowflake from behind the silken screen.

'No,' said the startled Mandarin.

'Tell my stonemasons,' said the whisper that was a falling drop of rain, 'to build our walls in the shape of a shining lake.'

The Mandarin said this aloud, his heart warmed.

'And with this lake of water,' said the whisper and the old man, 'we will quench the fire forever!'

The city turned out in joy to learn that once again they had been saved by the magnificent Emperor of ideas. They ran to the walls and built them nearer to this new vision, singing, not as loudly as before, of course, for they were tired, and not as quickly, for since it had taken a month to build the wall the first time, they had had to neglect business and crops and therefore were somewhat weaker and poorer.

There then followed a succession of horrible and wonderful days, one in another like a nest of frightening boxes.

'Oh, Emperor,' cried the messenger, 'Kwan-Si has rebuilt their walls to resemble a mouth with which to drink all our lake!'

'Then,' said the Emperor, standing very close to his silken screen, 'build our walls like a needle to sew up that mouth!'

'Emperor!' screamed the messenger. 'They make their walls like a sword to break your needle!'

The Emperor held, trembling, to the silken screen. 'Then shift the stones to form a scabbard to sheathe that sword!'

'Mercy,' went the messenger the following morn, 'they have worked all night and shaped their walls like lightning which will explode and destroy that sheath!'

Sickness spread in the city like a pack of evil dogs. Shops closed. The population, working now steadily for endless months upon the changing of the walls, resembled Death himself, clattering his white bones like musical instruments in the wind. Funerals began to appear in the streets, though it was the middle of summer, a time when all should be tending and harvesting. The Mandarin fell so ill that he had his bed drawn up by the silken screen and there he lay, miserably giving his architectural orders. The voice behind the screen was weak now, too, and faint, like the wind in the eaves.

'Kwan-Si is an eagle. Then our walls must be a net for that eagle. They are a sun to burn our net. Then we build a moon to eclipse their sun!'

Like a rusted machine, the city ground to a halt.

At last the whisper behind the screen cried out:

'In the name of the gods, send for Kwan-Si!'

Upon the last day of summer the Mandarin of Kwan-Si, very ill and withered away, was carried into our Mandarin's courtroom by four starving footmen. The two mandarins were propped up, facing each other. Their breaths fluttered like winter winds in their mouths. A voice said:

'Let us put an end to this.'

The old men nodded.

'This cannot go on,' said the faint voice. 'Our people do nothing but rebuild our cities to a different shape every day, every hour. They have no time to hunt, to fish, to love, to be good to their ancestors and their ancestors' children.'

'This I admit,' said the mandarins of the towns of the Cage, the Moon, the Spear, the Fire, the Sword and this, that, and other things.

'Carry us into the sunlight,' said the voice.

The old men were borne out under the sun and up a little hill. In the late summer breeze a few very thin children were flying dragon kites in all the colours of the sun, and frogs and grass, the colour of the sea and the colour of coins and wheat.

The first Mandarin's daughter stood by his bed.

'See,' she said.

'Those are nothing but kites,' said the two old men.

'But what is a kite on the ground?' she said. 'It is nothing. What does it need to sustain it and make it beautiful and truly spiritual?'

'The wind, of course!' said the others.

'And what do the sky and the wind need to make *them* beautiful?'

'A kite, of course – many kites, to break the monotony, the sameness of the sky. Coloured kites, flying!'

'So,' said the Mandarin's daughter. 'You, Kwan-Si, will make a last rebuilding of your town to resemble nothing more nor less than the wind. And we shall build it like a golden kite. The wind will beautify the kite and carry it to wondrous heights. And the kite will break the sameness of the wind's existence and give it purpose and meaning. One without the other is nothing. Together, all will be beauty and cooperation and a long and enduring life.'

Whereupon the two mandarins were so overjoyed that they took their first nourishment in days, momentarily were given strength, embraced, and

lavished praise upon each other, called the Mandarin's daughter a boy, a man, a stone pillar, a warrior, and a true and unforgettable son. Almost immediately they parted and hurried to their towns, calling out and singing, weakly but happily.

And so, in time, the towns became the Town of the Golden Kite and the Town of the Silver Wind. And harvestings were harvested and business tended again, and the flesh returned, and disease ran off like a frightened jackal. And on every night of the year the inhabitants in the Town of the Kite could hear the good clear wind sustaining them. And those in the Town of the Wind could hear the kite singing, whispering, rising, and beautifying them.

'So be it,' said the Mandarin in front of his silken screen.

Ray Bradbury

October, November, December,
Glow, like an ember,
Roast, warm as toast,
Heat your feet, under the sheet.